I Love kisses

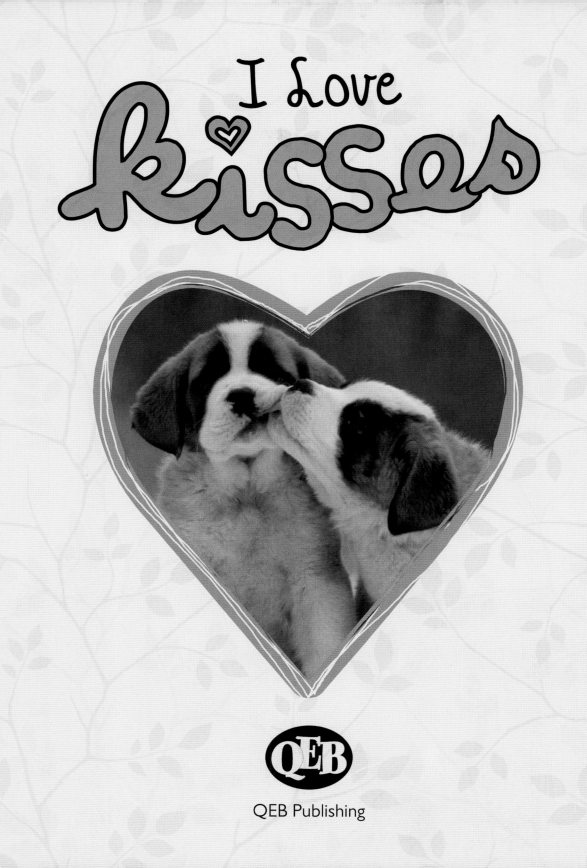

QEB

QEB Publishing

We love kisses,
and lots of animals
love kisses, too!

When someone kisses
you, it makes you
feel warm inside.

Animals kiss their
friends and their family.

A kiss is a wonderful way
to say hello or good-bye
and to show someone
that you love them.

Love can start with a kiss.

A little peck on the cheek shows someone that I like them.

When a male little owl wants to find a mate, he calls out with a soft "hoot." A pair of little owls often stays together for life, and they both take care of their chicks.

There is **always** time for a quick **KiSS** when I say **good-bye.** I'll be back after **playing** with my **friends.**

Bottlenose dolphins live in groups called pods. Newborns stay with their mother. When they are bigger, all of the young dolphins in the pod play and swim together.

Sometimes Mom feels sad or tired. We keep kissing her until she feels happy again!

Cheetahs are good mothers. They work hard to protect their cubs from hyenas, lions, and eagles, and to find food for the whole family.

When my family comes over, I get smothered with kisses.

Zebras live in family groups called herds. Aunts, cousins, and sisters often help take care of a baby zebra, called a foal. They like to make a fuss of a foal and nuzzle and nibble its face and neck!

I'd like to get to know you better, and a little kiss is my way of saying "hello!"

Tree frogs are busy at night, looking for food. If two strangers bump into each other, they touch noses. It's a good way to decide if they can become mates.

It's bathtime, and Mom is trying to clean me.

She gives me a kiss to make me sit still!

Gorillas love to spend hours grooming one another. A mother checks every part of her baby's body to make sure that there are no nasty bugs living on his or her skin.

Mom gives me a kiss before she leaves. When she comes back, she will have some tasty treats for me!

Harp seal pups have fluffy, white fur and cannot swim until they grow short, gray fur. Their mothers must leave them alone on the snow while they go off fishing.

It's time to go. Kiss me quick!

Impalas are antelopes from Africa. Even when they are sharing a special moment, they must stay alert and watch out for lions or other predators.

Sometimes we fight, but we always kiss and make up.

Rabbits, like many other animals, use smell to decide if another animal is a friend or an enemy. Touching noses and mouths are just two of the many ways that animals can show that they trust one another.

Dad has taken us swimming, and we are so tired! There's time for a sisterly kiss before we take a little nap.

Swan chicks are called cygnets, and their dad helps take care of them. He takes them to the river so that they can practice swimming. He might carry them on his back as he glides gracefully through the water.

I'm small and scared, but my mom's kisses make me feel big and brave.

A grizzly bear cub needs its mother. She feeds it and protects it from other bears, wolves, and cougars. A mother grizzly is a very dangerous animal when her cub is threatened.

A Kiss on the lips is lovely, but sneaky kisses are just as sweet!

A giraffe calf is about 7 feet tall and can run within one hour of being born. One mother takes care of a group of calves in a nursery, while the other mothers find food.

A kiss cheers me up when I'm feeling sad.

A pair of lovebirds spends their whole lives together. They like to sit close together and even nibble each other's beaks to show that they care!

Best friends love to share things, and a kiss is the perfect gift to give to that special someone.

Hippopotamuses are sociable animals. They live together in groups and often spend the day wallowing in pools to keep cool. At night, they leave the water to feed on grass.

Here are three good reasons for kissing.

A kiss is the shortest distance between two friends.

💜

Kisses are easy to give and lovely to get.

💜

A kiss is a gift of love.

Can you think of any more?

Editor: Tasha Percy
Designer: Natalie Godwin
Cover Designer: Krina Patel
Art Director: Laura Roberts-Jensen

Copyright © QEB Publishing 2014

First published in the United States in 2014 by
QEB Publishing
3 Wrigley, Suite A
Irvine, CA 92618

www.qed-publishing.co.uk

A CIP record for this book is available from the Library of Congress.

ISBN 978 1 60992 720 2

Printed in China

Picture credits
(t=top, b=bottom, l=left, r=right, c=center, fc=front cover)
1 Shutterstock:Gizele, 1c Getty:Minden Pictures:Mitsuaki Iwago, 2 FLPA:Minden
Pictures:Gerry Ellis, 3 Shutterstock:Sweet Lana, 4 Shutterstock:Daemys, 5 Naturepl.
com:Dietmar Nill, 6 Naturepl.com:Jeff Rotman, 7 Shutterstock:Markovka,
8 Shutterstock:EV-DA, 9 FLPA:Frans Lanting, 10 FLPA:Richard Du Toit
11 Shutterstock: yaskii, 12 Shutterstock:Sweet Lana, 13 Getty:JH Pete Carmichael,
14 Alamy:Dave Stevenson, 15 Shutterstock:WEN WEN, 16 istockphoto.
com:Electric Crayon, 17 Getty:Hiroya Minakuchi, 18 FLPA:Minden Pictures:Suzi
Eszterhas, 19 Shutterstock:Natalia Kudryavtseva, 20 Shutterstock:yaskii, 21
FLPA:Andrew Parkinson, 22 naturepl.com:Paul Hobson, 23 Shutterstock:Markovka,
24 istockphoto.com:Silmen, 25 Biosphoto:Michael Breuer, 26 Getty:Gail Shotlander,
27 Shutterstock:Gizele, 28 Shutterstock:Daemys, 29 Imagebroker:Michael Krabs,
30 Naturepl.com:Anup Shah, 31 Shutterstock:Natalia Kudryavtseva,
32 Shutterstock:Sweet Lana, 32t FLPA:Minden Pictures:Yva Momatiuk & John
Eastcott, fc Getty:Roland Weihrauch, bct Shutterstock:BerndtVorwald,
bcbl Shutterstock:Moolkum, bcbr Shutterstock: David Steele